King Benjamin Builds a Tower

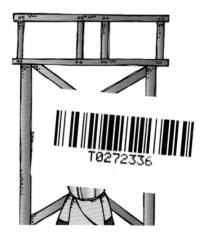

written by Tiffany Thomas
illustrated by Nikki Casassa

CFI · An imprint of Cedar Fort, Inc · Springville, Utah

HARD WORDS:
Benjamin, tower, families, Mosiah

PARENT TIP: Find a comfortable place to do your reading. Like the couch, the bed, or a soft chair.

King Benjamin leads
the people of Nephi.

King Benjamin
is a man of God.

King Benjamin wants to
talk to the people.

King Benjamin builds a tall tower.

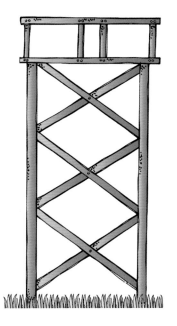

The people come to the tower.

They are in tents with their families.

King Benjamin
teaches the people.

The people listen.

The people want to get baptized.

King Benjamin is happy.
His son Mosiah is now the new king.

The people are happy.
King Mosiah is happy.

The end.

ISBN 13: 978-1-4621-4337-5

Published by CFI, an imprint of Cedar Fort, Inc. • 2373 W. 700 S., Suite 100, Springville, UT 84663
Distributed by Cedar Fort, Inc., www.cedarfort.com

Cover design and interior layout design by Shawnda T. Craig
Cover design © 2022 Cedar Fort, Inc.
Printed in China • Printed on acid-free paper
10 9 8 7 6 5 4 3 2 1